BOOK /

Written by

Translated b

Bridget
Jones's
Diary

BY HELEN FIELDING

Bright
≡**Summaries**.com

HELEN FIELDING

BRITISH NOVELIST AND JOURNALIST

- **Born in Morley (England) in 1958**
- **Notable works:**
  - *Cause Celeb* (1994), novel
  - *Bridget Jones's Diary* (1996), novel
  - *Olivia Joules and the Overactive Imagination* (2004), novel

After graduating with a degree in English from Oxford University, Helen Fielding worked as a journalist for the BBC. She then became a columnist for the newspaper *The Independent*, where she created the character of Bridget Jones. In 1994 she published her first novel, *Cause Celeb*. When *Bridget Jones's Diary* was published, the author achieved international success with this 'chick-lit' book that was loved by women across several generations.

The fact that Fielding is British is particularly noticeable in her cultural references, which include the novels of Emily Brontë (English writer, 1818-1848) and the presenters of British television programmes. Whatever the dramatic content of the subjects she deals with, the journalist always manages to evoke them with a touch of humour.

BRIDGET JONES

IN PRAISE OF AWKWARDNESS

- **Genre:** novel
- **Reference editions:**
  - Fielding, H. (1996) *Bridget Jones's Diary*. London: Picador.
  - Fielding, H. (1999) *Bridget Jones: The Edge of Reason*. London: Picador.
  - Fielding, H. (2013) *Bridget Jones: Mad About the Boy*. London: Jonathan Cape.
- **First editions:** 1996, 1999 and 2013
- **Themes:** social conventions, emotional relationships, feminism, addiction, working environment

Bridget Jones's Diary, which first appeared as a series in the British newspaper *The Independent* between 1995 and 1996, was published in full for the first time in 1996. The sequel, *The Edge of Reason*, appeared in 1999, while the third installment, *Mad About the Boy*, kept readers waiting and finally came out in 2013.

Presented as a private diary, these novels are narrated by a clumsy thirtysomething singleton from London who is desperately looking for love and inner harmony. Although the narrative tackles some distressing existential problems for a young woman at the end of the 20th century, the tone is light, original and irresistibly funny.

The first two volumes of this romantic saga achieved true

global success and were adapted for the big screen in 2001 and 2004.

SUMMARY

BRIDGET JONES'S DIARY

The novel opens with Bridget full of positive resolutions and reluctantly on her way to her family's traditional New Year's dinner. One of these resolutions is to keep a diary in which she will record her weight and the number of cigarettes, units of alcohol and calories she consumes each day. During the meal, pressured by her mother Pamela and her mother's friends, who want to see her fall into the arms of the rich divorced lawyer Mark Darcy, Bridget starts a conversation with this somewhat awkward man. Their encounter turns into a fiasco for the young thirtysomething.

Single, but terrified at the idea of ending up alone, Bridget fantasises about her boss, Daniel Cleaver, with whom she exchanges risqué messages at work. They embark on a tempestuous and unstable relationship in which neither of them seem to really know what they want. Daniel blows hot and cold, inundating Bridget with passionate messages before letting her down the next time they meet. She also involuntarily sends him mixed signals, not knowing what advice to follow between the practical guides she devours and the advice of her friends. This equivocation regarding the right attitude to adopt towards the men she lusts after will be a recurring theme in her diary.

Their relationship ends suddenly when Bridget discovers that Daniel is cheating on her with a thinner woman. The idea of playing hard to get therefore applies perfectly to their relationship, as he comes back to her repeatedly until they end up having sex one last time, when Daniel is drunk. Without him, our antiheroine lives more healthily: she officially gives up smoking and drinking, and she loses weight, a goal that she has had since the age of 18. Nonetheless, her friends think that she looks ill without these extra pounds. In any case, after a significant bout of depression, she returns to her usual weight and her bad habits.

Bridget's best friends also all experience romantic setbacks: the sweet Jude, who is going out with Vile Richard; the committed feminist Sharon; and Tom, the gay man who is in love with Pretentious Jerome. This is not a bad thing for Bridget, who is always delighted to forget about her own misery for a time in order to tend to other people's distress.

Meanwhile, Bridget's mother leaves her husband for a Portuguese man she met on holiday and becomes a presenter on a television programme for divorced women. In order to help her daughter forget about her ex-boyfriend Daniel, Pamela finds her a job as a journalist for a television channel. Bridget sees this as an opportunity to escape her horrible head of department, Perpetua, but also to get away from Daniel Cleaver and to flourish professionally by finally becoming a serious journalist. Nevertheless, the young woman soon becomes disillusioned. Her new boss Richard Finch, a notorious cocaine addict, constantly reprimands her for her repeated lateness and makes her do often ridiculous reporting, such as interviewing hunters while sitting backwards on a horse.

Although her professional career does not appear to be

taking off, Bridget's love life starts to look up when she gets to know Mark Darcy better thanks to her mother, who is arrested for joining her lover in Portugal after he has cheated her friends out of money. The lawyer manages to find the conman and gets him to come to the Jones's Christmas party by telling him that Pamela has gone back to her husband. When the lover arrives at the party, Mark has him arrested by the police and in this way saves Bridget's mother from going to prison. Once the police have left with the criminal, he whisks the young woman away from the terrible family meal, takes her out to dinner at a hotel and confesses his feelings for her, which turn out to be reciprocated.

BRIDGET JONES: THE EDGE OF REASON

Bridget and Mark's relationship, riddled with misunderstandings, faces numerous setbacks in the second volume of the saga, notably when the young woman receives love letters from an unknown person and when Rebecca, a friend of Mark's who is in love with him, plants doubt in his mind. Bridget suspects that he is refusing to commit, since while he is happy to spend the night at hers, he never returns the invitation. In reality, he doesn't like his house, which he finds sinister. After a series of misunderstandings, the couple end up breaking up, with Mark suspecting Bridget of infidelity. Some time after their separation, when he wants to give her a love letter he accidentally replaces his note with the transcription of a poem. This new confusion further sets back their reunion.

Beyond these misunderstandings, Mark feels that he always

comes after Bridget's friends and is being constantly analysed according to the advice in the practical guides that the young woman devours, such as *Men Are from Mars, Women Are from Venus* (book written by John Gray in 1992). When Bridget learns this, she decides to throw out all these books. Mark, who is walking past her house at that time, notices the mountain of books in the bin. In a twist of fate – or a twist by the author – while Bridget has got rid of all her manuals to try and win back Mark, he has had the opposite idea and got hold of as many practical guides as possible to find out how to win over Bridget again.

The saviour motif, which was present in the first volume, reappears here when Bridget is trapped by a trafficker and imprisoned in Thailand for drug trafficking. Mark gets her out of the situation and delivers the guilty party to the local authorities, which allows them to see each other again after their breakup. Shortly afterwards, after sending a letter to the workman who made a hole in the wall of her apartment threatening to take him to court if he doesn't make progress in his work, Bridget receives a bullet with her name carved on it from him. Mark makes her realise the danger she is in and takes her to the police station to file a report. To protect her, he lets her stay with him until the man is arrested. This is how the two lovebirds end up getting back together for good and admitting their love for one another again.

BRIDGET JONES: MAD ABOUT THE BOY

Bridget Darcy comes back to her diary after a decade of happiness and the birth of two children with Mark. He has died and she misses him terribly. During four long years of mourning, she puts on weight and becomes depressed, before feeling the woman who lies dormant inside her wake up, although not without a sense of guilt. Fortunately, her friends are still there, except Sharon, who now lives in America and is replaced by Talitha, an attractive cosmetic surgery aficionado in her sixties. They all want Bridget to lose her "Born-Again Virginity" (p. 187). Thanks to their helpful advice, the widow loses 20kg in an obesity treatment centre and, after a makeover, meets a man in a nightclub. They see each other twice, but Bridget is not ready for a new relationship and he stops calling her. She then signs up to dating sites and develops a Twitter addiction. A handsome thirtysomething, Roxby, then contacts her: they see each other for several months and Bridget manages to grieve Mark. However, they end up separating because she does not want to spoil her lover's youth. Feeling old after this episode, she decides to get Botox injections.

To regain control of her career, the widow attempts the theatrical adaptation of a play that she thinks is by Chekov (Russian writer, 1860-1904), but that turns out to be by Ibsen (Norwegian playwright, 1828-1906). After an initial meeting, her producer asks her to adapt the Norwegian script to the setting of Hawaii and ends up making her rewrite the entire story. Faced with this much popularisation, Bridget resigns. Over the course of these daily trials, she ends up throwing in the towel because she feels too vulnerable without Mark.

At the same time, she must also look after her children: their digestive disorders, their questions about their father, emails from school, numerous texts from the nanny, the arrogant criticisms from other students' mothers, etc. In spite of all that, little Mabel and Billy are her greatest joy. During a school concert, Mr Wallaker, Billy's gymnastics teacher, comes over to Bridget and tries to kiss her. Thinking that he is married, she rebuffs him. She learns that this is not the case thanks to a neighbour and, several months later, they fall in love and bring their families together, after Mr Wallaker saves Billy from an accident on a school trip. In this way, the saviour motif once again reappears successfully.

CHARACTER STUDY

BRIDGET JONES

A proud "Singleton" (*Bridget Jones's Diary*, Wednesday 1 February), Bridget is a thirtysomething, slightly chubby brunette who worries about her age and her body and is desperately looking for love and inner harmony. To this end, she tries to live a healthier life and scrupulously counts the number of cigarettes, units of alcohol and calories that she consumes each day. Nonetheless, this does not stop her from binge eating, becoming depressed about her weight and, sometimes, "chain-smoking butt ends" (*Bridget Jones's Diary*, Friday 28 April). She also keeps a record of the number of calls she receives, the number of times she checks who has called her, and even the number of seconds since she last had sex.

This last number can sometimes be astronomical, as Bridget has lots of difficulties in her relationships with men. She spends a lot of time thinking about the balance of power within couples and asking her friends how many days to wait before calling after a date so as not seem needy. These obsessive considerations thus reveal a real communication problem between the sexes at a time when women's liberation had overturned all the codes which governed their relationships. Because of these difficulties, she is truly obsessed with her phone and harbours "fears of dying alone and being found three weeks later half-eaten by an Alsatian" (*Bridget Jones's Diary*, Wednesday 4 January) without having found a man who is prepared to commit to and respect her.

This antiheroine who is always late, often because she was struggling to find clean clothes, makes our own imperfections seem less dramatic because of the silly, even ridiculous, situations she regularly finds herself in. There is a social gap between her and her parents, especially her mother. The latter is a socialite who frequents the Rotary Club, whereas Bridget is more or less middle class, buys her clothes from cheap shops and yet often finds herself without money. To begin with, she and the rich Mark Darcy experience a sort of culture shock when they start dating, because there is a real socio-economic difference between them. In this way, Fielding has created a sort of Everywoman in whom readers can easily recognise themselves. That said, the exaggeration of this antiheroine's faults also allows the reader to shed their own complexes since, no matter how awkward or badly organised they are, Bridget Jones can always do worse. This is the case, for example, in her work, where she puts off the tasks she needs to do for as long as she can, while at the same time dreaming of thriving professionally. There are two passages which are particularly comforting for readers: the one where Bridget hosts a dinner party and the colour runs from the string holding the mixed herbs together, turning her soup blue, and the one where, after putting several pans filled with food on the floor, she steps in one of them.

When she returns in the third book, Bridget recounts that, after talking at length about the independence of the modern woman in her first two diaries, she married Mark Darcy and stopped working to become a stay-at-home mother.

After her husband's death Bridget, who is now in her fifties and morally weakened, enters a long period of depression, which she eventually gets out of thanks to her children and her friends. Her children have become her reason for living and all their actions fill her with love. In spite of the trials she has faced, she has stayed true to herself and has not made much progress with regard to organisation, housekeeping, discipline at her new job, or her relationships with men.

MRS PAMELA JONES

Bridget's mother always achieves what she sets out to do, even if this means disregarding information which doesn't suit her. A woman of the world and a stickler for convention, she endlessly scolds Bridget about her single status, assisted in this by her friends who try to push Bridget into the arms of a range of single men. Animated by a sort of late mid-life crisis subtly influenced by feminism, Pamela leaves her husband to host a television programme aimed at divorced women with a taste for drama. When she returns home following an escapade in Portugal with her conman lover, she accompanies Mr Jones when he enters rehab for alcoholism, where her overflowing self-confidence unsettles all the hospital staff. Although she interferes in Bridget's life with all sorts of absurd recommendations, she sometimes manages to genuinely help her, as in the case of Mark. In the third volume, now a widow, Pamela goes to live with her friend Una in a luxury care home, where she still charms men her age.

MR COLIN JONES

Bridget's father is her ally and her partner in crime in the face of her mother's joyful tyranny. After the indignities that his wife makes him undergo, from the Portuguese lover in the first book to the Kikuyu guest she brings back from holiday in the second volume, he gradually fades away and finds refuge in whisky, to the despair of his daughter, whom he sometimes calls drunk in the middle of the night and who is worried about him.

DANIEL CLEAVER

A "bloody bastard" (*Bridget Jones's Diary*, Saturday 13 May), sleazy, chauvinist and alcoholic, Daniel is Bridget's boss at the start of her adventures. When they date, he personifies to some extent the dark side of the young woman. Indeed, as he is a character driven by pleasure, their relationship is based primarily on physical relations: they drink, smoke and have sex together. After they break up, he sometimes re-enters the fray, much to Mark Darcy's displeasure. However, in the third book he makes amends and becomes the godfather of the Darcy children. He sometimes looks after them, stuffing them with sweets and making an indescribable mess in the house. Still partial to drink, he will end up going to rehab twice.

MARK DARCY

A world-renowned lawyer specialising in human rights, rich, divorced and gentlemanly, Mark is the archetype of the ideal man and the complete opposite of Daniel. This character represents the knight in shining armour, a motif which Helen Fielding draws on a lot. He is drawn to the originality of Bridget, whose awkwardness and unconventionality charm him because they distinguish her in his eyes from other women. Bridget feels at ease with him and, after his death, misses the humour, security and comfort which surrounded her when he was alive.

THE "URBAN SINGLETON FAMILY" (*THE EDGE OF REASON*)

Fortunately, whatever happens Bridget can always find comfort by smoking and drinking Chardonnay with her friends, or spend hours talking on the phone with them about the approach to take with their respective conquests.

- **Sharon.** For this enthusiastic disciple of feminist essays, men represent the enemy. She is therefore always the first to criticise them and, in particular, those who break up with her friends. In spite of this, in the third book she moves to America to live with a man she met on the internet.
- **Jude.** Sweet and addicted to love, this expert in international economics marries Vile Richard, to the great displeasure of Sharon, who nonetheless serves as maid of honour alongside Bridget. They subsequently divorce, and at the end of the novels Jude, who is now around 50, is still looking for her soulmate.
- **Tom.** Gay, but still subject to heartbreak, this psychologist has a nose job after a painful breakup.

- **Talitha.** Bridget's former colleague appears in *Mad About the Boy*. She is a sensual woman in her sixties, and regularly has cosmetic surgery to preserve her looks.

ANALYSIS

WOMEN'S WRITING

Bridget Jones's Diary and the television series *Sex and the City* (adapted from the novel by the American journalist Candace Bushnell) both appeared in the middle of the 1990s and are considered the founding works of a genre known as "chick lit", which is seen as being the exclusive preserve of women. This vaguely feminist literature deals with women's problems in a fairly direct way. The heroines of the genre recount, often in the first person and always with humour, their lives as women, with all the clichés that this entails: emotional turmoil and the professional setbacks of women who are not taken seriously, expensive shopping sprees and the organisation of dinner parties – which, in the case of the clumsy Bridget Jones, never go to plan.

However, Bridget differs from the usual "chick lit" formula because, an antiheroine par excellence, she is not glamorous. She buys her clothes from Marks and Spencer rather than from luxury stores and, above all, she is clumsy, often short of money, disorganised and sometimes even dirty. In short, she is more in keeping with the reality of the middle class than with the perfect, wealthy, conventional, Gucci-clad heroines of *The Devil Wears Prada* (novel by the American author Lauren Weisberger, published in 2005) or *Desperate Housewives* (American television series, 2004-2012). Moreover, in the third book, the work moves away from the detached tone of "chick lit" and its fashion dramas to deal with a real tragedy: the death of Mark Darcy. This change of tone somewhat shocked fans, because it broke to a certain degree with the lightness and the principle of "all's well that ends well" which governed the first two volumes. Even if it has changed, the basic blueprint nonetheless remains present, notably thanks to the return of another stereotype: the knight in shining armour, which recurs in Fielding's novels. The heroine can always count on a powerful male to get her out of trouble, whether she is imprisoned, threatened or in the middle of trying to save her son from a car accident.

THE PRIVATE DIARY FORM

The work is presented in the form of a private diary and contains many characteristics of the genre.

- The book is written in the first person singular, which allows us to directly enter the inner turmoil of the main character. This approach allows us to identify fairly easily with Bridget and at the same time to profoundly grasp her erratic character, which is amplified by the sometimes disjointed and over-the-top presentation of her train of thought. For example, here is the introduction to the first day of her diary: "9st 3 (but post-Christmas), alcohol units 14 (but effectively covers 2 days as 4 hours of party was on New Year's Day), cigarettes 22, calories 5424."
- The narrator is intradiegetic: she is a participant in the narrative.
- The novel first appeared as a weekly column in the newspaper *The Independent*. This pace of distribution suits the form of *Bridget Jones's Diary* and gives it a realistic dimen-

sion, as if the narrator were really delivering an account of her day each week. Moreover, this makes the reader feel a sense of anticipation as they look forward to seeing the next issue and with it the next part of the novel.

- The private diary is a written work in which the narrator records on a more or less regular basis their state of mind and the events taking place in their life. The antiheroine opens her notebooks almost every day to write about her life and ask herself questions about it. But these serious headaches about her future and her love life are always with the lightness of humour, which stops this inner questioning from appearing too gloomy.

A CRITICAL REFLECTION ON SOCIETY

By virtue of its focalisation on a gaffe-prone antiheroine, *Bridget Jones's Diary* presents, in a roundabout way, a critique of society and the conventions which govern it, whether in regard to romantic relationships, social events or philosophical opinions.

The questioning of social conventions

Bridget regularly questions the unwritten rules which govern human relationships. She never knows what to say or do at parties or on dates, she doesn't know when she should call a man or wait for him to call, she doesn't know how to use Twitter properly, etc. Because of this, she reads lots of how-to guides and often consults her friends to try and discover the correct way to behave; most of the time she is unsuccessful in this. As well as love affairs, the work examines interpersonal relationships more generally, whether these are between friends, as shown in the conflicts between Bridget and her friends, or family members, as suggested by, for example, Pamela Jones's attitude towards her daughter when she is going through problems.

A certain feminism

Although Sharon and Bridget claim to be feminists, the latter would be completely unable to clearly define this movement. However, the approach to the difference between the sexes gives the novel an undeniable feminist dimension, even if it is confused and sometimes impeded by the attitude of the female characters. We can note Bridget's contradictory reactions to men, as she claims that she can do without them but at the same time doggedly pursues them.

Obsessions and addictions

This theme is always present in the background, between the antiheroine who is constantly trying to fight her dependence on tobacco, white wine and unhealthy food, and two of her loved ones who end up in rehab. Without losing its humorous tone, the series goes further in describing Bridget's obsessive behaviours, as she sometimes checks her letter box and the calls she has received dozens of times a day.

Relationships at work

The protagonist's questions about the development of her career and her unpleasant relationships with some coworkers in the three jobs she holds successively evoke, under the guise of humour, another problem in our society, namely harassment at work, whether this is psychological or sexual.

A SERIES IN THE VEIN OF THE WORKS OF JANE AUSTEN

The first two volumes of *Bridget Jones's Diary* make repeated explicit references to the Jane Austen (British author, 1775-1817) novel *Pride and Prejudice* (1813).

- Bridget and her friends Judith and Sharon truly worship the television adaptation of the novel, which they watch some parts of on a loop during their parties while fantasising about the hero Mr Darcy. The latter's surname is identical to that of the heroine's future husband. Indeed, Bridget herself points this out before remarking on the similarity of their characters: "It struck me as pretty ridiculous to be called Mr Darcy and to stand on your own looking snooty at a party" (*Bridget Jones's Diary*, Sunday 1 January). Furthermore, they are both rich and could be described as "good matches". Bridget further increases the confusion between the two characters when she goes to Rome to interview the actor Colin Firth, who plays the hero in the series of the Austen novel and has such an effect on her as Mark Darcy.
- The nod to this classic of English literature even extends to the storyline of the novel. The heroines of both works are single women of a certain age – in relation to the norms of their respective societies – who risk ending up as old maids and are subjected to the power of an authoritarian mother who wants to marry them to a rich man.

Likewise, Fielding's heroine becomes infatuated with a former friend of Mark Darcy, Daniel Cleaver, who is just as treacherous and perverse as Austen's Mr Wickham. Both men stir up mistrust in the heroine towards their rival, and romantic misunderstandings are as present between Mark and Bridget as between Mr Darcy and Elizabeth.

- In both novels, the heroine reconsiders her dislike for the hero after he saves, in Bridget's case, her mother Pamela, and in Elizabeth's case her sister, sparing the former from the dishonour of prison and the latter from the dishonour of adultery.
- In terms of ideas, both works present a critique of the customs and behaviours of the society around them, mainly with regard to the position of women and the role of marriage in their social and moral status. They also both extensively evoke the power plays that are present in interpersonal relationships, both social and romantic.

FURTHER REFLECTION

SOME QUESTIONS TO THINK ABOUT...

- Bridget often mentions her phone and, later on, her computer and social networks. How could her relationship with technology be described?
- In your opinion, why does the widowed Bridget only open her diary again after Mark's death?
- In what way do Helen Fielding's writing and the use of the private diary form contribute to the representation of the erratic character of the heroine and her adventures?
- In an interview with *Vogue*, Helen Fielding explained: "there's a tragicomic element in my writing; the happy ending is just where you choose to end a book. Life, with all its twists and turns, carries on beyond it." How would you apply this comment to the books?
- "Feeling much better now. Have realized answer is not to obsess about own problems but help others" (*The Edge of Reason*). How do you understand this kind of remark from the heroine?
- Bridget proclaims that she is a "singleton" and a "feminist". Explain in what way(s) she adheres to these concepts.
- Bridget's two best friends are Sharon, who represents the modern feminist woman, and Jude, who is sensitive and reflects more traditional values such as commitment and marriage. What position does the heroine occupy in these ideological conflicts, and in what way are they compatible or incompatible?
- Bridget's failure to conform to social norms is not always

by choice. Explain this with the help of examples.

- In what way can this nonconformist attitude be compared to other heroines from the genre, such as Carrie Bradshaw in *Sex and the City* or Andy Sachs in *The Devil Wears Prada*?
- Explain why, in your opinion, Bridget does not realise that she is exceptional.

We want to hear from you!
Leave a comment on your online library
and share your favourite books on social media!

FURTHER READING

REFERENCE EDITIONS

- Fielding, H. (1996) *Bridget Jones's Diary*. London: Picador.
- Fielding, H. (1999) *Bridget Jones: The Edge of Reason*. London: Picador.
- Fielding, H. (2013) *Bridget Jones: Mad About the Boy*. London: Jonathan Cape.

REFERENCE STUDIES

- Guerin, M. (2013) Mort de Mark Darcy: Helen Fielding nous dit pourquoi. *Elle*. [Online]. [Accessed 23 December 2015]. Available from: <http://www.elle.be/fr/11407-mort-mark-darcy-helen-fielding-dit.html>
- Lane, T. (2005) Women's lives are reflected in 'chick lit' genre. *The Blade*. [Online]. [Accessed 21 October 2016]. Available from: <http://www.toledoblade.com/Books/2005/11/13/Women-s-lives-are-reflected-in-chick-lit-genre.html>
- Peras, D. (2006) La "chick lit": les dernières tendances. *L'Express*. [Online]. [Accessed 26 December 2015]. Available from: <http://www.lexpress.fr/culture/livre/la-chick-lit-les-dernieres-tendances_811248.html>

ADDITIONAL SOURCES

- Silverman, R. (2013) Bridget Jones: is Helen Fielding's own loss the reason for Mark Darcy's death? *The Telegraph*. [Online]. [Accessed 10 October 2016].

Available from: <<http://www.telegraph.co.uk/culture/>
<books/10350708/Bridget-Jones-is-Helen-Fieldings-own->
<loss-the-reason-for-Mark-Darcys-death.html>>

ADAPTATIONS

- *Bridget Jones's Diary*. (2001) [Film]. Sharon Maguire. Dir. United States/United Kingdom: StudioCanal.
- *Bridget Jones: The Edge of Reason*. (2004) [Film]. Beeban Kidron. Dir. United States/United Kingdom: StudioCanal.

9575081R00020

Printed in Germany
by Amazon Distribution
GmbH, Leipzig